Inspirations

Our greatest gift is not in never falling but in rising every time we fall.

When making your choice in life, do not neglect to live.
Samuel Johnson (1709 - 1784)

Along with success comes a reputation for wisdom.
Euripides

Where is there dignity unless there is honesty?
Cicero

Give all to love; obey thy heart.
Ralph Waldo Emerson (1803 - 1882)

Choose a job you love, and you will never have to work a day in your life.
Confucius

The secret to happiness is not in doing what one likes to do, but in liking what one has to do.
Anonymous

The magic of first love is our ignorance that it can ever end.
Benjamin Disraeli

At the touch of love everyone becomes a poet.
Plato

Cherish your visions and your dreams, as they are the children of your soul; the blueprints of your ultimate achievements.
Anonymous

The soul should always stand ajar, ready to welcome the ecstatic experience.
Dickinson, Emily (1830 - 1886)

Without friends no one would choose to live, though he had all other goods.
Aristotle (384 BC - 322 BC)

A wise man will make more opportunities than he finds.
Sir Francis Bacon (1561 - 1626)

Do not forget to entertain strangers, for by so doing some have unwittingly entertained angels.
[Hebrews 13:2] Bible

There is nothing as strong as tenderness,
And nothing as tender as true strength.
Saint Francis de Sales

A journey of a thousand miles begins with a single step.
Lao-Tzu (604 BC - 531 BC)

I never saw an ugly thing in my life: for let the form of an object be what it may - light, shade, and perspective will always make it beautiful.
John Constable (1776 - 1837)

If we could see the miracle of a single flower clearly, our whole life would change.
Buddha

We all have strength enough to endure the misfortunes of others.
Francois de La Rochefoucauld

Action is eloquence.
William Shakespeare (1564 - 1616)

Keep your fears to yourself, but share your courage with others.
Robert Louis Stevenson (1850 - 1894)

You cannot depend on your eyes when your imagination is out of focus.
Mark Twain (1835 - 1910)

However brilliant an action, it should not be esteemed great unless the result of a great motive.
Francois de La Rochefoucauld,

A life of peace, purity, and refinement leads to a calm and untroubled old age.
Cicero

Whatever you are, be a good one.
Abraham Lincoln (1809 - 1865)

Don't worry if you're a kleptomaniac, you can always take something for it.
Unknown

Shun idleness. It is a rust that attaches itself to the most brilliant of metals.
Voltaire (1694 – 1778)

To love oneself is the beginning of a life-long romance.
Oscar Wilde (1854 - 1900)

Every new beginning comes from some other beginning's end.
Seneca

Every man's life is a fairy-tale written by God's fingers.
Hans Christian Andersen (1805 - 1875)

The greatest of faults, I should say, is to be conscious of none.
Thomas Carlyle

These things I command you, that ye love one another.
John 15:17

The worst solitude is to be destitute of sincere friendship.
Sir Francis Bacon

All truths are easy to understand once they are discovered; the point is to discover them.
Galileo Galilei

Let not your heart be troubled.
Bible, John xiv. 1.

A smile is a light in the window of the soul indicating that the heart is home.
Anonymous

A happy life consists in tranquillity of mind.
Cicero

To understand the heart and mind of a person, look not at what he has already achieved, but at what he aspires to do.
Kahlil Gibran

When I let go of what I am, I become what I might be.
Lao-Tzu (604 BC - 531 BC)

Never discourage anyone... who continually makes progress, no matter how slow.
Plato

Don't waste yourself in rejection, nor bark against the bad, but chant the beauty of the good.
Ralph Waldo Emerson (1803 - 1882)

I cannot say whether things will get better if we change; what I can say is they must change if they are to get better.
Georg Christoph Lichtenberg (1742 - 1799)

I hear and I forget. I see and I remember. I do and I understand.
Confucius

The cautious seldom err.
Confucius

Imagination rules the world.
Napoleon Bonaparte

My religion is very simple. My religion is kindness.
The Dalai Lama

It is not the strongest of the species that survive, nor the most intelligent, but the one most responsive to change.
Charles Darwin (1809 - 1882)

Knowledge is like a garden; if it is not cultivated, it cannot be harvested.
African Proverb

The wisest men follow their own direction.
Euripides

Blessed are the merciful; for they shall obtain mercy.
[Mathew] Bible

Nothing can bring you peace but yourself.
Ralph Waldo Emerson (1803 - 1882)

Good friends are like stars...you don't always see them, but you know they're always there.
Anonymous

Pleasure in the job puts perfection in the work.
Aristotle (384 BC - 322 BC)

Think only of the past as its remembrance gives you pleasure.
Jane Austen (1775 - 1817)

The secret of success is constancy of purpose.
Benjamin Disraeli

To keep the body in good health is a duty. . . otherwise we shall not be able to keep our mind strong and clear.
Buddha

A friend's eye is a good mirror.
Celtic Proverb

Discretion in speech is more than eloquence.
Sir Francis Bacon

A joy that's shared is a joy made double.
English Proverb

Happiness is like a butterfly. The more you chase it, the more it eludes you. But if you turn your attention to other things, It comes and sits softly on your shoulder.
Anonymous

Before we set our hearts too much upon anything, let us examine how happy those are who already possess it.
Francois de La Rochefoucauld

Hide not your talents, they for use were made. What's a sun-dial in the shade?
Benjamin Franklin

The only gift is a portion of thyself.
Ralph Waldo Emerson (1803 - 1882)

What the imagination seizes as beauty
must be the truth.
John Keats (1795 - 1821)

It is well to give when asked, but it is
better to give unasked, through
understanding.
Kahlil Gibran

Love is the beauty of the soul.
St. Augustine

Happiness is not given but exchanged.
Anonymous

When you encounter difficulties and
contradictions, do not try to break them,
but bend them with gentleness and time.
Saint Francis de Sales

When the character of a man is not clear to
you, look at his friends.
Japanese Proverb

Conquering others takes force, conquering yourself is true strength.
Lao-Tzu (604 BC - 531 BC)

He who hesitates is lost.
Proverb

Wealth maketh many friends.
[Proverbs 19:4] Bible

There are two mistakes one can make along the road to truth, not going all the way, and not starting.
Buddha

The journey is the reward.
Chinese Proverb

Let us be grateful to people who make us happy: They are the charming gardeners who make our souls blossom.
Marcel Proust (1871 - 1922)

The shifts of Fortune test the reliability of friends.
Cicero

All action is of the mind and the mirror of
the mind is the face, its index the eyes.
Cicero

Everything has its beauty but not
everyone sees it.
Confucius

As a man thinks in his heart, so is he.
[Proverbs 23:7].

If you do not hope, you will not find what is
beyond your hopes.
St. Clement of Alexandra

A love that can last forever takes but a
second to come about.
Cuban Proverb

We turn not older with years, but newer
every day.
Emily Dickinson

Cheese, wine, and a friend must be old to
be good.
Cuban Proverb

The greatest good you can do for another is not just share your riches, but reveal to them their own.
Benjamin Disraeli

A good name is rather to be chosen than great riches.
Proverbs, 22. 1

Courage and perseverance have a magical talisman, before which difficulties disappear and obstacles vanish into air.
John Quincy Adams (1767 - 1848)

True happiness... arises, in the first place, from the enjoyment of one's self.
Joseph Addison (1672 - 1719)

Never go to excess, but let moderation be your guide.
Cicero

You cannot dream yourself into a character; you must hammer and forge yourself one.
James A. Froude (1818 - 1894)

Wisdom outweighs any wealth.
Sophocles

Beauty is truth, truth beauty. That is all ye
know, and all ye need to know.
John Keats (1795 - 1821)

Kindness is the noblest weapon to conquer
with.
American Proverb

Sow to the wind and you will reap a
whirlwind.
Bible

Start by doing what's necessary; then do
what's possible; and suddenly you are
doing the impossible.
St. Francis of Assisi

Do not protect yourself by a fence, but
rather by your friends.
Czech Proverb

Energy and persistence conquer all things.
Benjamin Franklin

'Tis better to have loved and lost
Than never to have loved at all.
Alfred Lord Tennyson

The optomist sees the rose and not its
thorns; the pessimist stares at the thorns,
oblivious of the rose.
Kahlil Gibran

Never live in the past but always learn
from it.
Unknown

Well done is better than well said.
Benjamin Franklin

It is a rough road that leads to the heights
of greatness.
Seneca

Our waking hours form the text of our
lives, our dreams, the commentary.
Anonymous

And you will know the truth, and the truth will make you free.
[John 8:32]

It has been my experience that folks who have no vices have very few virtues.
Abraham Lincoln (1809 - 1865)

Remember that what you believe will depend very much on what you are.
Noah Porter (1811 - 1892)

Life itself can't give you joy, unless you really will it. Life just gives you time and space, it's up to you to fill it.
Anonymous

The appearance of right oft leads us wrong.
Horace

If you don't know where you are going, any road will take you there.
Lewis Carroll (1832 - 1898)

Happiness depends upon ourselves.
Aristotle (384 BC - 322 BC)

Let not a man guard his dignity, but let his dignity guard him.
Ralph Waldo Emerson (1803 - 1882)

We have all a better guide in ourselves, if we would attend to it, than any other person can be.
Jane Austen, Mansfield Park

A friend is, as it were, a second self.
Cicero

The real voyage of discovery consists not in seeking new landscapes, but in having new eyes.
Marcel Proust

A big shot is a little shot that kept shooting.
Anonymous

Far better a neighbour that is near than a
brother far off.
Bible

Our greatest glory is not in never falling,
but in rising every time we fall.
Confucius

Yesterday is but a dream, and tomorrow is
only a vision, but today well lived makes
every yesterday a dream of happiness and
every tomorrow a vision of hope.
Anonymous

Dignity consists not in possessing honors,
but in the consciousness that we deserve
them.
Aristotle (384 BC - 322 BC)

The greatest danger for most of us is not
that we aim too high and we miss it, but we
aim too low and reach it.
Michelangelo

Hope is the dream of the waking man.
French Proverb

In necessary things, unity; in doubtful things, liberty; in all things, charity.
Richard Baxter (1615 - 1691)

It's never too late to be who you might have been.
George Eliot (1819 - 1880)

One can acquire everything in solitude - except character.
Marie Henri Beyle (1783 - 1842)

Strong reasons make strong actions.
William Shakespeare (1564 - 1616)

Nothing great was ever achieved without enthusiasm.
Ralph Waldo Emerson (1803 - 1882)

Our truest life is when we are in dreams awake.
Henry David Thoreau (1817 - 1862)

Work spares us from three evils: boredom, vice, and need.
Voltaire (1694 – 1778)

Inspirations

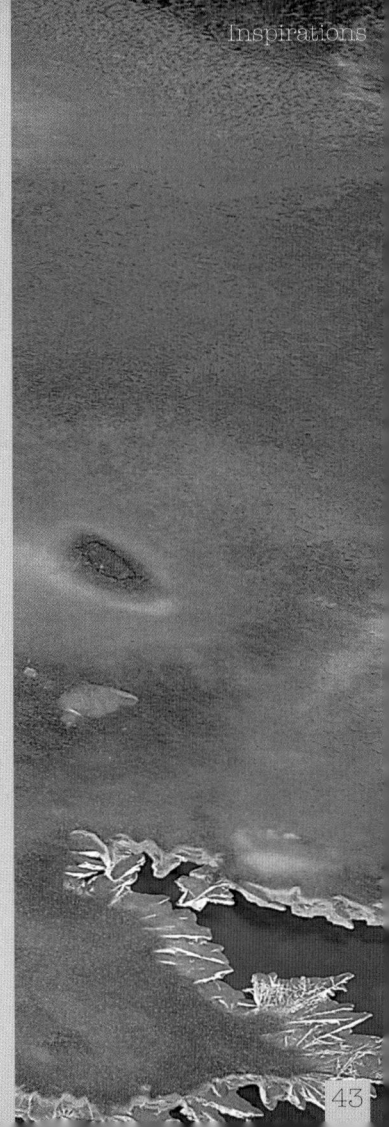

Wisdom is better than wit, and in the long run will certainly have the laugh on her side.
Jane Austen (1775 - 1817)

Never leave that 'til tomorrow which you can do today.
Benjamin Franklin

Fortune helps the brave.
Terence (185 BC - 159 BC), Phormio

Whoever does not love his work cannot hope that it will please others.
Unknown

Time eases all things.
Sophocles

Kindness in words creates confidence. Kindness in thinking creates profoundness. Kindness in giving creates love.
Lao-Tzu (604 BC - 531 BC)

Thy word is a lamp to my feet, and a light to my path.
[Psalm 119:105].

When I was a child, I spoke as a child, I thought as a child: but when I became a man I put away my childish things.
[I Corinthians] Bible

He that is of a merry heart hath a continual feast.
Proverbs, 15. 15

Govern thy life and thoughts as if the whole world were to see the one, and read the other.
Thomas Fuller (1608 - 1661)

Gratitude is not only the greatest of virtues, but the parent of all others.
Cicero

Ever has it been that love knows not its own depth until the hour of separation.
Kahlil Gibran

Better by far you should forget and smile than you should remember and be sad.
Christina Rossetti (1830 - 1894)

What you do not want done to yourself, do not do to others.
Confucius

Let the beauty of what you love, be what you do.
Rumi

Appreciation is a wonderful thing: It makes what is excellent in others belong to us as well.
Voltaire (1694 – 1778)

A loving heart is the truest wisdom.
Charles Dickens

The man who moves a mountain begins by carrying away small stones.
Confucius (551 BC - 479 BC)

One word frees us of all the weight and pain of life: That word is love.
Sophocles

It is easier to be wise for others than for ourselves.
Francois De La Rochefoucauld

Never refuse any advance of friendship,
for if nine out of ten bring you nothing, one
alone may repay you.
Madame de Tencin (1681 - 1749)

Advice is judged by results, not by
intentions.
Cicero

He who knows that enough is enough will
always have enough.
Lao-Tzu (604 BC - 531 BC)

Show Class, have pride and display
character. If you do, winning takes care of
itself.
Anonymous

The pleasure of love is in loving.
Francois de La Rochefoucauld

The only thing to do with good advice is
pass it on. It is never any use to oneself.
Oscar Wilde (1854 - 1900)

The entire law is summed up in a single command, "Love your neighbor as yourself."
Galatians 5:14 (NIV)

What would be the use of immortality to a person who cannot use well a half an hour.
Ralph Waldo Emerson (1803 - 1882)

Genius is eternal patience.
Michelangelo

Early to bed and early to rise makes a man healthy, wealthy, and wise.
Benjamin Franklin

Man is what he believes.
Anton Chekhov (1860 - 1904)

Unless you believe, you will not understand.
Saint Augustine (354 AD - 430 AD),
De Libero Arbitrio

Necessity, who is the mother of invention.
Plato

A man's true wealth is the good he does in the world. Beauty is eternity gazing at itself in a mirror. But you are eternity and you are the mirror.
Kahlil Gibran

There is calmness to a life lived in Gratitude, a quite Joy.
Anonymous

Self-confidence is the first requisite to great undertakings.
Samuel Johnson (1709 - 1784)

Ask, and it shall be given you; Seek, and ye shall find; Knock, and it shall be opened unto you.
Bible, New Testament, Matthew 7:7

Wisdom is the principal thing; therefore get wisdom; and with all thy getting get understanding.
Proverbs, 4. 7

The world belongs to the energetic.
Ralph Waldo Emerson (1803 - 1882)

...the goodness of the will depends on the intention of the end.
Saint Thomas Aquinas

Take good hold of instruction and don't let her go, keep her for she is your life.
Bible

To be content with what one has is the greatest and truest of riches.
Cicero

Reflect on your present blessings, of which every man has many; not on your past misfortunes, of which all men have some.
Charles Dickens (1812 - 1870)

Be not ashamed of mistakes and thus make them crimes.
Confucius

I can do all things through Christ who strengthens me.
Philippians 4:13

Don't walk behind me, I may not lead.
Don't walk in front of me, I may not follow.
Just walk beside me and be my friend.
Unknown

Wherever there is a human being, there is
an opportunity for kindness.
Seneca

The things we know best are the things we
haven't been taught.
Marquis de Vauvenargues (1715 - 1747)

Fortune favours the brave.
Virgil (70 BC - 19 BC)

Rarely do great beauty and great virtue
dwell together.
Petrarch (1304 - 1374)

To travel hopefully is a better thing than to
arrive, and the true success is to labour.
Robert Louis Stevenson (1850 - 1894)

Friends have all things in common.
Plato

A word of encouragement during a failure is worth more than an hour of praise after success.
Anonymous

You can search throughout the entire universe for someone who is more deserving of your love and affection than you are yourself, and that person is not to be found anywhere. You yourself, as much as anybody in the entire universe deserve your love and affection.
Buddha

A true friend is the greatest of all blessings, and that which we take the least care of all to acquire.
Francois de La Rochefoucauld (1613 - 1680)

With most men, unbelief in one thing springs from blind belief in another.
Georg Christoph Lichtenberg (1742 - 1799)

There is no duty more obligatory than the repayment of kindness.
Cicero

What we call pleasure, and rightly so is the absence of all pain.
Cicero

A person's true wealth is the good he or she does in the world.
Mohammed

That is true wisdom, to know how to alter one's mind when occasion demands it.
Terence

Where there is hatred, let me sow love. Where there is injury, pardon. Where there is doubt, faith.
Saint Francis of Assisi

Put more trust in nobility of character than in an oath.
Solon (638 BC - 559 BC)

It is more blessed to give than to receive.
Bible, Acts xx. 35.

One should always play fairly when one has the winning cards.
Oscar Wilde (1854 - 1900)

Divide each difficulty into as many parts as necessary to resolve it.
Descartes

Go confidently in the direction of your dreams. Live the life you have imagined.
Henry David Thoreau (1817 - 1862)

As a general rule the most successful man in life is the man who has the best information.
Benjamin Disraeli (1804 - 1881)

Good, better, best; never let it rest till your good is better and your better is best.
Anonymous

We are what we repeatedly do. Excellence, then, is not an act, but a habit.
Aristotle (384 BC - 322 BC)

Everybody likes to go their own way--to choose their own time and manner of devotion.
Jane Austen, Mansfield Park

Giving up doesn't always mean you are weak...sometimes it means that you are strong enough to let go.
Unknown

Better a diamond with a flaw than a pebble without.
Confucius

Character is like a tree and reputation like its shadow. The shadow is what we think of it; the tree is the real thing.
Abraham Lincoln (1809 - 1865), Lincoln's Own Stories

Every artist was first an amateur.
Ralph Waldo Emerson (1803 - 1882)

Keep cool and you command everybody.
Louis de Saint-Just (1767 - 1794)

If you have knowledge, let others light their candles at it.
Margaret Fuller (1810 - 1850)

Much speech is one thing, well-timed speech is another.
Sophocles

The reward of a thing well done is to have done it.
Ralph Waldo Emerson (1803 - 1882)

Those who love deeply never grow old.
Anonymous

What lies behind us and what lies before us are tiny matters compared to what lies within us.
Ralph Waldo Emerson (1803 - 1882)

Science is organized knowledge. Wisdom is organized life.
Immanuel Kant

Our thoughts are free.
Cicero

The man of wisdom is never of two minds;
the man of benevolence never worries;
the man of courage is never afraid.
Confucius

Curiosity is, in great and generous minds,
the first passion and the last.
Samuel Johnson

Seek not happiness too greedily, and be
not fearful of happiness.
Lao-Tzu (604 BC - 531 BC)

A real friend is one who walks in when the
rest of the world walks out.
Anonymous

You cannot plough a field by turning it
over in your mind.
Author Unknown

Where is there dignity unless there is
honesty?
Cicero (106 BC - 43 BC)

He that can have patience can have what he will.
Benjamin Franklin

Tenderness and kindness are not signs of weakness and despair, but manifestations of strength and resolutions.
Kahlil Gibran (1883 - 1931)

What lies behind us and what lies before us are tiny matters compared to what lies within us.
Ralph Waldo Emerson (1803 - 1882)

The superior man is modest in his speech, but excels in his actions.
Confucius (551 BC - 479 BC)

What we anticipate seldom occurs; what we least expected generally happens.
Benjamin Disraeli

Without an acquaintance with the rules of propriety, it is impossible for the character to be established.
Confucius (551 BC - 479 BC)

If a man will begin with certainties, he shall end in doubts; but if he will be content to begin with doubts he shall end in certainties.
Sir Francis Bacon

There is no fear in love; but perfect love casteth out fear.
Bible, 1 John iv. 18.

The only lasting beauty is the beauty of the heart.
Rumi

Only actions give life strength; only moderation gives it a charm.
Jean Paul Richter (1763 - 1825)

Have patience with all things, but chiefly have patience with yourself. Do not lose courage in considering you own imperfections but instantly set about remedying them - every day begin the task anew.
Saint Francis de Sales

Judge not according to appearance, but judge righteous judgment.
Bible

Let bravery be thy choice, but not bravado.
Menander (342 BC - 292 BC)

Be great in act, as you have been in thought.
William Shakespeare (1564 - 1616)

Never promise more than you can perform.
Publilius Syrus

Time is the most valuable thing a man can spend.
Theophrastus

Do unto others as you would have others do unto you.
[Matthew 7:120] Bible

The best way to cheer yourself up is to try to cheer someone else up.
Mark Twain (1835 - 1910)

The absolute good is not a matter of opinion but of nature.
Cicero

If you have knowledge, let others light their candles at it.
Margaret Fuller (1810 - 1850)

Much speech is one thing, well-timed speech is another.
Sophocles

A kind heart is a fountain of gladness, making everything in its vicinity freshen into smiles.
Washington Irving

We are brought nothing into this world, and it is certain we can carry nothing out.
Bible

Goals that are not written down are just wishes.
Anonymous

It does not matter how slowly you go, so long as you do not stop.
Confucius

We need never be ashamed of our tears.
Charles Dickens

So long as we are loved by others I should say that we are almost indispensable; and no man is useless while he has a friend.
Robert Louis Stevenson

An investment in knowledge always pays the best interest.
Benjamin Franklin

Patience is the companion of wisdom.
Saint Augustine

Remember when life's path is steep to keep your mind even.
Horace

Little minds are tamed and subdued by misfortune; but great minds rise above it.
Washington Irving

Blessed is the influence of one true, loving human soul on another.
George Eliot (1819 - 1880)

Don't be too timid and squeamish about your actions. All life is an experiment. The more experiments you make the better.
Ralph Waldo Emerson (1803 - 1882)

Happiness comes through doors you didn't even know you left open.
Anonymous

Nurture your mind with great thoughts; to believe in the heroic makes heroes.
Benjamin Disraeli

Remember not only to say the right thing in the right moment, but far more difficult, is to leave unsaid the wrong thing in the tempting moment.
Benjamin Franklin (1706 - 1790)

Courage is resistance to fear; mastery of fear - not absence of fear.
Mark Twain

Life is a journey, and love is what makes
that journey worthwhile.
Unknown

Wisdom is better than rubies.
Proverbs, 8. 11.

In attempts to improve your character,
know what is in your power and what is
beyond it.
Francis Thompson (1859 - 1907)

Make all you can, save all you can, give all
you can.
John Wesley (1703 - 1791)

Hope is a waking dream.
Aristotle (384 BC - 322 BC)

The timeless in you is aware of life's
timelessness; and knows that yesterday is
but today's memory and tomorrow is
today's dream.
Kahlil Gibran

I believe that every human mind feels pleasure in doing good to another.
Thomas Jefferson (1742 - 1826)

If there is anything better than to be loved it is loving.
Anonymous

Wheresoever you go, go with all your heart.
Confucius

Humor is the great thing, the saving thing. The minute it crops up, all our irritations and resentments slip away and a sunny spirit takes their place.
Mark Twain (1835 - 1910)

All glory comes from daring to begin.
William Shakespeare (1564 - 1616)

The ornament of a house is the friends who frequent it.
Ralph Waldo Emerson (1803 - 1882)

When you meet your antagonist, do everything in a mild and agreeable manner. Let your courage be as keen, but at the same time as polished, as your sword.
Richard Brinsley Sheridan (1751 - 1816)

To the world you may be one person, but to one person you may be the world.
Anonymous

Don't let what you can't do interfere with what you can do.
Anonymous

The face is the mirror of the mind, and eyes without speaking confess the secrets of the heart.
Saint Jerome

Nature herself makes the wise man rich.
Cicero

In order to discover new lands, one must be willing to lose sight of the shore for a very long time.
Anonymous

Shallow men believe in luck. Strong men believe in cause and effect.
Ralph Waldo Emerson (1803 - 1882)

To be able under all circumstances to practice five things constitutes perfect virtue; these five things are gravity, generosity of soul, sincerity, earnestness and kindness.
Confucius

Love is a canvas furnished by Nature and embroidered by imagination.
Voltaire (1694 - 1778)

One cannot answer for his courage when he has never been in danger.
Francois de La Rochefoucauld

Life is a play. It's not its length, but its performance that counts.
Seneca

Life without love is a shadow of things that might be.
Unknown

Things do not change; we change.
Henry David Thoreau (1817 - 1862)

Make the most of yourself, for that is all
there is of you.
Ralph Waldo Emerson (1803 - 1882)

Our span of life is brief, but is long enough
for us to live well and honestly.
Cicero

Friendship is certainly the finest balm for
the pangs of disappointed love.
Jane Austen, Northanger Abbey

Knowledge is power.
Sir Francis Bacon

The greatest pleasure in life is doing what
people say you cannot do.
Walter Bagehot (1826 - 1877)

As is a tale, so is life, not how long it is, but
how good it is, is what matters.
Seneca

Happiness resides not in posessions and not in gold; the feeling of happiness dwells in the soul.
Democritus

Success is counted sweetest by those who ne'er succeed.
Emily Dickinson

Next to knowing when to seize an opportunity, the most important thing in life is to know when to forego an advantage.
Benjamin Disraeli

And in the sweetness of friendship let there be laughter and the sharing of pleasures. For in the dew of little things the heart finds its morning and is refreshed.
Kahlil Gibran

There is no fear in love; but perfect love casteth out fear ...
John 4:18

Manifest plainness,
Embrace simplicity,
Reduce selfishness,
Have few desires.
Lao-Tzu (604 BC - 531 BC)

A friend is someone who knows the song in
your heart, and can sing it back to you
when you have forgotten the words.
Anonymous

It is not because things are difficult that
we do not dare, it is because we do not dare
that they are difficult.
Seneca

We must walk consciously only part way
toward our goal and then leap in the dark
to our success.
Henry David Thoreau (1817 - 1862)

Respect yourself and others will respect
you.
Confucius

This edition published in 2008 by Bizzybee Publishing Ltd. Text by Melanie Shaw.
© bizzybee publishing 2008 Printed in China